ON TOP OF OLD SMOKY

A Collection of Songs and Stories from Appalachia

ON TOP OF OLD SMOKY

A Collection of Songs and Stories from Appalachia

Compiled and adapted by
Ronald Kidd

With pictures by
Linda Anderson

Ideals Children's Books • Nashville, Tennessee

Cover illustration: **At the Foot of Mount Yonah,** from the artist's collection. Photo by Richard Smith.
Back cover illustration: **The Quilters III,** from the artist's collection. Photo by Richard Smith.

Text in this format copyright © 1992 by Ideals Publishing Corporation
Illustrations copyright © 1992 by Linda Anderson

All rights reserved. No part of this publication may be reproduced or
transmitted in any form or by any means, electronic or mechanical,
including photocopy, recording, or any information storage and retrieval
system, without permission in writing from the publisher.

Published by Ideals Publishing Corporation
Nashville, Tennessee 37214

Printed and bound in Mexico.

ISBN 0-8249-8586-9 (lib. book)
ISBN 0-8249-8569-9 (tr. book)
ISBN 0-8249-7513-8 (book/cassette package)

Library of Congress Cataloging-in-Publication Data

Kidd, Ronald.
On top of Old Smoky: a collection of songs and stories from
Appalachia/compiled and adapted by Ronald Kidd; with pictures by
Linda Anderson.
p. cm.
Summary: A collection of eleven traditional songs and three folk
tales from Appalachia, including "The Frog He Went A'Courting,"
"I Gave My Love a Cherry," and "Jack and the Bean Tree."
ISBN 0-8249-8586-9 (lib. bdg.)—ISBN 0-8249-8569-9 (trade)
1. Folk songs, English—Appalachian Region—Texts. 2. Tales—
Appalachian Region. [1. Folk songs—Appalachian Region. 2. Folklore—
Appalachian Region.] I. Anderson, Linda. 1941- ill. II. Title.
PZ8.3.K5360n 1992 782.42162'21074—dc20 92-14437 CIP AC

The illustrations in this book were rendered in oil paints on Belgium linen
and in oil crayons on fine-grit sandpaper.
The display type was set in Caslon Antique.
The text type was set in Galliard.
Color separations were made by Web Tech, Inc.
Printed and bound by R.R. Donnelley & Sons.

Designed by Stacy Venturi-Pickett.

Introduction

Imagine leaving your home and your country and, together with your family and friends, moving to a new land. It is a beautiful place—but rugged and wild. There are few people and fewer roads. There is no television, nor even many books. The only thing you have for entertainment is each other. So during the long afternoons and evenings, you gather to share stories and songs from your homeland.

That is what happened to a widely scattered group of English, Scottish, and Irish people who came to America during the 1700s and 1800s. They settled in Appalachia, the mountainous region which stretches from southwestern Pennsylvania, through western Maryland, the Virginias, Kentucky, Tennessee, and the Carolinas, to northern Georgia and northeastern Alabama.

The settlers brought with them a rich tradition of folksongs and stories from the British Isles, and in the centuries that followed, they passed this valuable heritage down to their children, grandchildren, and great-grandchildren.

Early in the 1900s, folklore experts visited Appalachia and discovered the widespread popularity of tales and tunes from Great Britain. A number of the songs and stories had not been heard in the British Isles for over a hundred years, while others were still well-known in England—and some songs had even become popular throughout America. Yet the versions found in Appalachia were different. Cut off from the rest of the United States, these mountain people had developed their own tradition by adapting the words and music to fit their unique style of speaking and singing.

On Top of Old Smoky is a collection of Appalachian songs and stories adapted from accounts of some of the earliest folklore experts to visit this region. As you read and listen, remember the people who left home to settle those wild, rugged mountains, bringing their heritage with them.

—Ronald Kidd

The Frog He Went A-Courting

The frog he went a-courting, he did ride,
   Uh-huh.
The frog he went a-courting, he did ride,
   Uh-huh.
The frog he went a-courting, he did ride,
With a sword and pistol by his side,
   Uh-huh, uh-huh, uh-huh.

He rode up to Miss Mouse's door
Where he had never been before.

Says, "Miss Mouse, won't you marry me?"
"No, not if Uncle Rat don't agree."

Uncle Rat went a-running down to town
To get his niece a wedding gown.

The frog would laugh and shake his sides
To think that a mouse would be his bride.

Oh, what will the wedding supper be?
Three green beans and a black-eyed pea.

The first to come in was a bumblebee
With his fiddle on his knee.

The next to come in was an old fat goose.
He began to fiddle and she got loose.

The next to come in was an old tomcat.
He says, "I'll put a stop to that."

The goose, she flew up on the wall.
And the old tomcat put a stop to it all.

On Top of Old Smoky

On top of old Smoky, all covered with snow,
I lost my true lover by sparking too slow.

For sparking is pleasure, and parting is grief,
And a false-hearted lover is worse than a thief.

It's a-raining, it's a-hailing, the moon gives no light,
Your horses can't travel this dark, lonesome night.

Go put up your horses, and feed them some hay;
Come sit down here by me as long as you stay.

My horses aren't hungry, they won't eat your hay,
So farewell my darling, I'll feed on my way.

I'll drive on to Georgia, I'll write you my mind;
My mind is to marry and leave you behind.

Your parents are against me, and mine are the same.
If I'm down in your book, love, please rub off my name.

I'll go up old Smoky, on the mountain so high,
Where the wild birds and turtledoves can hear my sad cry.

Winter Snowfall, from the Bank South collection. Photo by Anthony Blair.

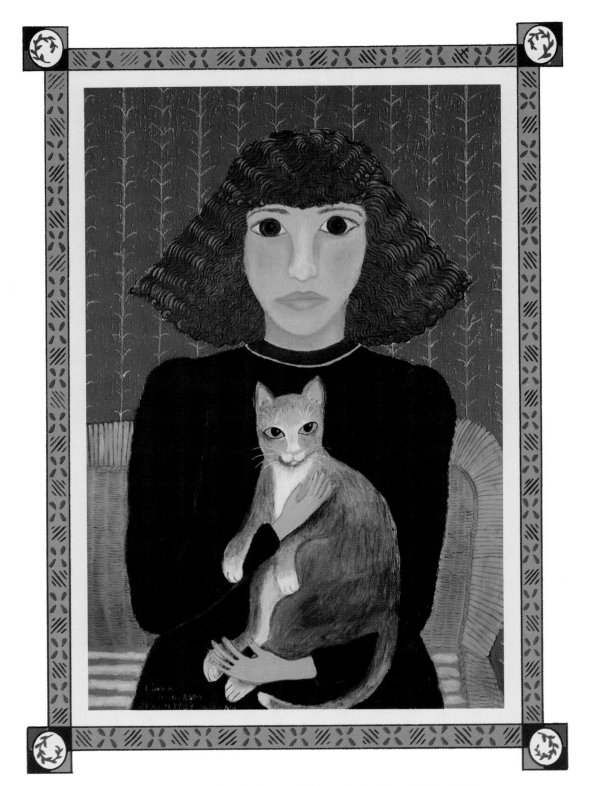

Annmarie and Her Cat, from the Annmarie Anderson collection. Photo by Richard Smith.

Billy Boy

Oh, where have you been,
Billy boy, Billy boy,
Oh, where have you been, charming Billy?
I have been to seek a wife
For the pleasures of my life;
She's a young thing
And cannot leave her mammy.

Did she ask you to come in,
Billy boy, Billy boy,
Did she ask you to come in, charming Billy?
Yes, she asked me to come in,
There's a dimple on her chin,
She's a young thing
And cannot leave her mammy.

Can she make a chicken pie,
Billy boy, Billy boy,
Can she make a chicken pie, charming Billy?
She can make a chicken pie
Till it makes the preachers cry,
She's a young thing
And cannot leave her mammy.

Can she card and can she spin,
Billy boy, Billy boy,
Can she card and can she spin, charming Billy?

She can card and she can spin,
She can do most anything,
She's a young thing
And cannot leave her mammy.

Can she sew and can she fell,
Billy boy, Billy boy,
Can she sew and can she fell, charming Billy?
She can sew and she can fell,
She can use her needle well,
She's a young thing
And cannot leave her mammy.

How tall is she, Billy boy, Billy boy,
How tall is she, charming Billy?
She's as tall as any pine,
And as slim as a pumpkin vine,
She's a young thing
And cannot leave her mammy.

How old is she, Billy boy, Billy boy,
How old is she, charming Billy?
She's twice six and twice seven,
Twenty-eight and eleven;
She's a young thing
And cannot leave her mammy.

Jack and the Bean Tree

Once there was a boy named Jack who lived with his granny, and they had a little place back up in a holler.

Now, one morning, Jack's granny was sweeping the house, and she swept up a bean. She said, "Here, boy, take this bean outside and plant it, and make you a bean tree." Jack did what she told him to then went off to play.

Well sir, the next morning he ran out early to see about his bean tree, and what do you think? It had grown to the top of the house! Jack ran inside and cried, "Granny, my bean tree is as high as the house!"

She said, "Go on out of here, boy. You know it's not up yet."

A while later she went outside, and sure enough it was as high as the house. It made her kind of sorry that she hadn't believed Jack, so she gave him a piece of bread and butter with brown sugar.

The next morning Jack jumped up again and ran outside. He came back a minute later, and he called, "Granny, my bean tree's as high as the sky!"

"Son," she says, "don't come in here telling such lies as that. You know it's not as high as the sky."

After a while, when she got through with her cleaning, she went outside, and sure enough, that bean tree had grown right up through the clouds. She felt bad, so she gave Jack a big slice of cake and some sweet milk.

The next morning, there was no stopping Jack. He ran straight out of the house and went to climbing that bean tree. He told Granny, "I'll hack you off a mess of beans on my way up." So he climbed and climbed and threw her down some beans. And after a while he made it to the top.

Jack hopped off and got to wandering around a field till he reached a great big house. A woman was sitting on the porch, and she said, "Law, little boy, what are you doing here? Don't you know my husband's a giant? He eats all the Englishmen he finds."

A Mill in North Georgia, from the Boyd Anderson collection.

Jack got to shaking and said, "Oh, hide me, please, hide me." So she hid him under the bed. Directly the old giant came in and yelled, "Fi fo fiddle-dee fun, I smell the blood of an Englishman! Dead or alive, I'll have his bones to eat with my bread and butter."

His wife said, "Aw now, poppy, don't talk that way. That was just a little old poor boy that was here this evening, and he's gone now."

So the giant ate his supper while Jack stayed under the bed. While that boy lay there, he noticed a brass candlestick and decided he wanted it. After supper, the giant and his wife fell asleep, and Jack eased out and got the candlestick, and down the bean tree he went.

Jack rested the next day, but the morning after that, he climbed up the bean tree again. He went to the giant's house, and the giant's wife said, "Law, boy, what did you come back for? The giant knows somebody stole his candlestick, and he'll sure eat you up."

"No, he won't," said Jack. "Just let me hide under the bed one more night." So she let him crawl under there. Pretty soon the giant came in and said, "Fi fo fiddle-dee fun, I smell the blood of an Englishman! Dead or alive, I'll have his bones to eat with my bread and butter."

"Aw, poppy," said his wife, "don't talk that way. It was just that little old poor boy that was here again."

The giant looked around some, but he didn't look under the bed. After a while, he got tired of that and sat down to supper, and pretty soon he and his wife went to sleep and were snoring again.

Jack, he lay there and studied what he'd get next, and he noticed the giant had slipped off his boots. So way in the night, Jack crawled out and got the boots and went down the bean tree just as fast as he could go.

This time Jack rested two or three days, but he still wanted to go back. So the next morning, he climbed up the bean tree and went to the giant's house. When the giant's wife saw him, she said, "Law, boy, the giant's awfully mad. Somebody stole his boots. You better go away before he catches you and eats you up."

"Aw, he won't catch me," said Jack. "Just let me come in one more time." So she let him do it. Directly the giant came home and said, "Fi fo fiddle-dee fun, I smell the blood of an Englishman. Dead or alive I'll have his bones to eat with my bread and butter."

"Law, now, poppy," said his wife, "that little old poor boy's been here, but he's not coming back again."

The giant looked around the house, but he didn't look under the bed. After supper, the giant and his wife fell asleep, just like before. This time, Jack peeked out from under the bed and saw the prettiest little china bells fastened to the bed cords. He started untying the bells, and every now and then one would jingle, and the giant would roll over in his sleep. Finally Jack got them all untied and started running for the bean tree, and the china bells started to jingle something awful.

The giant sat up in his bed and said, "Fi fo fiddle-dee fun, I smell the blood of an Englishman. Dead or alive I'll have his bones to eat with my bread and butter." And he took out after Jack.

When Jack got to the bean tree, he climbed down, then he looked up and saw the giant coming right after him.

Jack hollered, "Give me a hand ax, Granny! Give me a hand ax!"

She did, and Jack began to hack and hack. Down came the bean tree, and it took the better part of an hour to fall. When it hit the ground, you can bet that was the end of that old giant.

A Woman and Her Birds, from the Mr. and Mrs. David Gambrell collection. Photo by Richard Smith.

The Cuckoo

Now, the cuckoo is a pretty bird; she sings as she flies.
She brings us sweet tidings; she tells us no lies.
She sucks the pretty flowers to keep her voice clear,
She never says "cuckoo" till summer is near.

Come all you young girls, take warning by me;
Never place your affections on a sycamore tree.
The leaves, they will welter, the roots will run dry,
My true love's forsaken me, and I cannot tell why.

My true love's forsaken me, I'm sure he's foresworn;
He's badly mistaken if he thinks that I'll mourn.
I'll do unto him as he's done unto me;
I'll get another sweetheart, and that you'll all see.

I Gave My Love a Cherry

I gave my love a cherry that had no stones,
I gave my love a chicken that had no bones,
I gave my love a ring that had no end,
Oh, I gave my love a baby with no crying.

How can there be a cherry that has no stones?
How can there be a chicken that has no bones?
How can there be a ring that has no end?
How can there be a baby with no crying?

A cherry when it's blooming, it has no stones,
A chicken when it's pipping, it has no bones,
A ring when it's rolling, it has no end,
A baby when it's sleeping, there's no crying.

Levi Tomlin's, from a private collection. Photo by Gary Bogue.

The Green Grass Grew All Around

There was a tree up in the woods,
The prettiest tree that you ever did see.
Oh, the tree in the woods,
And the green grass grew all around and
around, the green grass grew all around.

And on that tree, there was a limb,
The prettiest limb that you ever did see.
Oh, the limb on the tree, and the tree in
the woods,
And the green grass grew all around and
around, the green grass grew all around.

And on that limb, there was a twig,
The prettiest twig that you ever did see.
Oh, the twig on the limb, and the limb
on the tree, and the tree in the woods,
And the green grass grew all around and
around, the green grass grew all around.

And on that twig, there was a nest,
The prettiest nest that you ever did see.
Oh, the nest on the twig, and the twig on
the limb, and the limb on the tree, and
the tree in the woods,
And the green grass grew all around and
around, the green grass grew all around.

And in that nest, there was an egg,
The prettiest egg that you ever did see.
Oh, the egg in the nest, and the nest on
the twig, and the twig on the limb, and
the limb on the tree, and the tree in the
woods,
And the green grass grew all around and
around, the green grass grew all around.

And in that egg, there was a bird,
The prettiest bird that you ever did see.
Oh, the bird in the egg, and the egg in
the nest, and the nest on the twig, and
the twig on the limb, and the limb on the
tree, and the tree in the woods,
And the green grass grew all around and
around, the green grass grew all around.

And on that bird, there was a feather,
The prettiest feather that you ever did see.
Oh, the feather on the bird, and the bird
in the egg, and the egg in the nest, and
the nest on the twig, and the twig on the
limb, and the limb on the tree, and the
tree in the woods,
And the green grass grew all around and
around, the green grass grew all around.

Catching Lightning Bugs, from the Michael Braff collection. Photo by Gary Bogue.

Jack and the Varmints

One day Jack was a-walking the road, whittling with his knife and making him a paddle. He came along past a mudhole where there were a bunch of little old blue butterflies. So he struck down with his paddle, and he killed seven of the butterflies.

He went on a piece further and came to a blacksmith shop, and he got the blacksmith to cut letters in his belt that said, "Look at that Jack—killed seven at a whack."

Now the king lived around there, and when Jack passed by, the king ran out and said, "I see you're a very brave man and killed seven at a whack."

"Yes, bedads," said Jack, "I'm a mighty brave man."

The king said, "Stranger, I want to hire a brave man to kill some varmints we have here in the woods. We have a wild municorn killing so many livestock; soon they'll all be dead. If you kill that municorn, we'll pay you one thousand dollars—five hundred now and five hundred when you bring the municorn in."

Jack said, "All right," and the king paid him five hundred dollars.

Jack went off to find the wild municorn, but on the way, he got to thinking how dangerous that municorn must be. "They'll never see me around here again," he said to himself, and he took out into the mountains.

But the municorn smelt Jack and followed him, and pretty soon here it came, *whippity cut, whippity cut, whippity cut.*

Jack took to running, and the municorn came after him. They ran up the mountains and down the ridges. Late in the evening, they started down a long ridge, and a-way down at the end of the ridge, Jack saw a big oak, and he made a beeline to see if he could climb it. When Jack shinnied up that oak, the municorn kept going and stove his horn into the trunk. The municorn rared and plunged, but Jack saw that it was fastened for all time to come.

Thunderstorm in the Jungle, from the Dick and Linda Cravey collection. Photo by Richard Smith.

Jack went back to the king's house, and the king said, "Did you get the municorn?"

"Municorn?" said Jack. "Law me, never was nothing but a little old bull calf. I just picked it up by one ear and tail and stove it against a tree, and if you all want it, you'll have to go up there and get it." So the king got him a great army and went up and killed the municorn.

The king came back and paid Jack five hundred dollars more and said, "Now Jack, there's another varmint living up there; a wild bull-boar that's been tearing up my settlement and killing lots of sheep. I'll give you five hundred dollars now and five hundred more if you kill that boar."

Jack took the five hundred dollars and said to himself, "You'll never see me around these parts anymore."

But after he'd gone a little ways, here came the wild boar after him, *whippity cut, whippity cut, whippity cut.*

All day long that boar chased him across the mountains and down the ridges—all the day, just a-running. Along late in the evening, a-way down in a holler, he saw an old house with no roof on it. The door was open, so Jack ran right inside and climbed up the wall, and when the boar followed him in, Jack hopped down outside, pushed the door to, and propped it shut with some timbers.

He went back to the king's house, and the king said, "Did you get the wild boar?"

"Wild boar?" said Jack. "Law me, I never saw nothing but a little old pig come bristling up after me. I just picked it up by the tail and threw it in an old house. If you want it, you'll have to go up there and get it." So the king got up an army of men, and they went up and killed the wild boar.

The king came back and paid Jack his other five hundred dollars, then

said, "Now Jack, there's one more varmint giving us trouble. It's a lion that's come over the mountains from Tennessee, and it's been killing cattle and horses and everything it comes across. I'll give you five hundred dollars now and five hundred more if you can kill it."

Jack said to himself, "If I can just get out of here, no lion will ever see me." He went a-way up on the mountain, but that old lion smelt him, and here it came, *whippity cut, whippity cut, whippity cut.*

Jack ran across the hills, up the ridges, and every which way, and the lion was right after him.

Late in the evening, a-way down at the end of a ridge, Jack saw an old pine tree that had been burnt over and was right black. Jack made a beeline for the tree and ran up it, and that made the old lion so mad that it started gnawing on the trunk. It gnawed and it gnawed.

Jack figured his only chance was to slip down and get away when the lion wasn't looking, so he eased down little by little. He was nearly to the bottom when he put his foot on a rotten limb. The limb broke, and Jack fell just a-straddle that old lion, and the lion took off.

Jack was a-hollering and screaming, and directly he ran the lion right through the town. The king's men saw the lion coming, and one of them grabbed his rifle and drew a bead on the lion and tumbled him up.

Well sir, Jack jumped to his feet, and he was a-swearing and a-raring. "See here, King," he said, "I caught your lion, and I was just riding it down here to get it broke in for you a-ridey horse, and now your men have done shot it."

When the king heard that, he raised a rumpus with his men and made them pay Jack the other five hundred dollars, plus a thousand more for ruining his lion.

Jack was rich when I left there, and I don't think he's worked any yet.

The Cat Went Fiddle-de-dee

Had me a cat; the cat pleased me.
Fed my cat under yonder tree;
   The cat went fiddle-de-dee.

Had me a dog; the dog pleased me.
Fed my dog under yonder tree;
The dog went bow-wow-wow,
   And the cat went fiddle-de-dee.

Had me a hen; the hen pleased me.
Fed my hen under yonder tree;
The hen went cluck-cluck,
The dog went bow-wow-wow,
   And the cat went fiddle-de-dee.

Had me a hog; the hog pleased me.
Fed my hog under yonder tree;
The hog went krusi-krusi,
The hen went cluck-cluck,
The dog went bow-wow-wow,
   And the cat went fiddle-de-dee.

Had me a sheep; the sheep pleased me.
Fed my sheep under yonder tree;
The sheep went baa-baa,

The hog went krusi-krusi,
The hen went cluck-cluck,
The dog went bow-wow-wow,
   And the cat went fiddle-de-dee.

Had me a cow; the cow pleased me.
Fed my cow under yonder tree;
The cow went moo-moo,
The sheep went baa-baa,
The hog went krusi-krusi,
The hen went cluck-cluck,
The dog went bow-wow-wow,
   And the cat went fiddle-de-dee.

Had me a calf; the calf pleased me.
Fed my calf under yonder tree;
The calf went maa-maa,
The cow went moo-moo,
The sheep went baa-baa,
The hog went krusi-krusi,
The hen went cluck-cluck,
The dog went bow-wow-wow,
   And the cat went fiddle-de-dee.

Catty and Vermin, from the Susan Shlaer collection. Photo by Richard Smith.

Hush, Little Baby

Hush, little baby, don't say a word,
Papa's gonna buy you a mockingbird.

If it can't whistle and it can't sing,
Papa's gonna buy you a diamond ring.

If that diamond ring turns to brass,
Papa's gonna buy you a looking glass.

If that looking glass gets broke,
Papa's gonna buy you a billy goat.

If that billy goat won't pull,
Papa's gonna buy you a cart and bull.

And if that cart and bull fall down,
You'll still be the prettiest girl around.

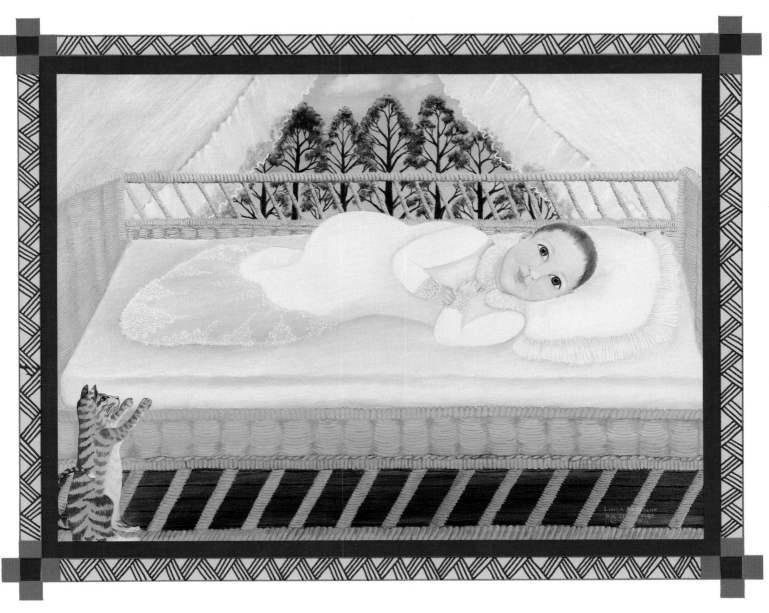

Baby in a Wicker Crib, from the Mr. and Mrs. David Kahn collection. Photo by Richard Smith.

Jack and the Cat

There was an old man who had three sons—Will, Tom, and Jack. Now, one day the old man called his boys together and told them to go off and see who could marry the richest girl. He offered to give his boys every penny he had, and Will and Tom took him up on it right quick. But that Jack, he was different. He said to his daddy, "I don't want but one thing you've got, and that's your old pet fox." And so the old man gave it to him.

The day they left, Will and Tom got themselves all dressed up fine, but they didn't let Jack follow them because he looked so bad. So Jack set off by himself.

Jack tramped across the country all day, and finally along about dark he saw a farmhouse. He thought he'd better go there and try to get lodging for the night. Didn't have a penny—just that old pet fox.

Jack went to the door and hollered, and out came the prettiest little cat. Jack hollered again, "Who keeps house here?"

The cat said, "Cat and mouse."

"Law me," said Jack, "a cat that talks!"

"I used to be a woman," said the cat, "but the witches got mad at me and witched me into a cat. If you'll stay here three days and nights and not let a thing come into this house, not the least little thing even down to a mouse, I'll turn into a pretty girl, and I'll marry you."

Jack squeezed the old fox, and the fox said, "Gold enough."

"Yes, bedads, I will," Jack told the cat. He put down the fox and whittled a big club and fixed himself at the door.

Cat Fight, from the Dick and Marianne Lambert collection. Photo by Richard Smith.

The first night, sure enough, elephants and bears and every kind of big critter came up the steps and tried to get in, and old Jack kept them away with his club.

When the sun rose up the next morning, the cat was bigger, and it looked a little bit like a girl. Jack ate some breakfast, and then he went out and whittled a middle-size club and fixed himself at the door.

The second night, here come all kinds of snakes and weasels and middle-size critters. It was a sight in the world how he went after them, and nary a one went through that door.

When the sun came up, the cat right favored a girl, but she still had claws and whiskers and cat ears. For breakfast, Jack went out and picked a mess of huckleberries, then he whittled a little paddle and some swatters and fixed himself at the door.

The third night, all sorts of spiders and hornets and little old things swarmed up and tried to go through the door, but Jack swatted every last one.

When the sun came up, there standing in the farmhouse was the prettiest little girl he ever did see. And for miles around the place there were livestock like chickens and sheep and horses, and fields that were just a-busting with crops.

"You sure beat that witch," said the girl. "For being so brave, everything around here is yours."

"Including you?" asked Jack.

"I reckon so," she said.

Jack picked up the old fox and squeezed it. "Gold enough," said the fox.

They got married the next day. The morning after that, Jack hitched up the horses and carriage, and they started out for his daddy's place to show him his new wife.

When they got near, they heard some banjo and fiddle music. Jack stopped the carriage and told his wife to wait there for him. He changed back into his old raggedy clothes and took the fox and walked up to his daddy's place.

Well sir, he found Jack's daddy there with Will and Tom and their new wives, playing some music. When they saw Jack, they commenced to laughing because of his raggedy old clothes, but Jack didn't pay them no mind. He just squeezed the old fox, and the fox said, "Gold enough."

Then Jack went back to his carriage and put on his good clothes. He tucked the old fox under his arm and drove back with his wife. When Jack's brothers saw the fancy carriage a-coming, all they could do was stare.

Jack got out of the carriage and said "hello" to Will and Tom and his daddy. He squeezed down on the old fox, and the fox said to the brothers, "Gold enough, but none for you."

Then Jack took his wife and they went on back, and when I left there, they were plumb rich and living happy.

Early in the Morning

This is the way we wash our clothes,
Wash our clothes, wash our clothes.
This is the way we wash our clothes,
Early Monday morning.

This is the way we iron our clothes,
Iron our clothes, iron our clothes.
This is the way we iron our clothes,
Early Tuesday morning.

This is the way we go to the store,
Go to the store, go to the store.
This is the way we go to the store,
Early Wednesday morning.

This is the way we patch our clothes,
Patch our clothes, patch our clothes.
This is the way we patch our clothes,
Early Thursday morning.

This is the way we sweep our floor,
Sweep our floor, sweep our floor.
This is the way we sweep our floor,
Early Friday morning.

This is the way we bake our bread,
Bake our bread, bake our bread.
This is the way we bake our bread,
Early Saturday morning.

This is the way we go to church,
Go to church, go to church.
This is the way we go to church,
Early Sunday morning.

Drying Apples, from the John and Sue Wieland collection. Photo by Richard Smith.

Black Is the Color

Black is the color of my true love's hair,
Her face is like some rosy fair;
The prettiest face and the neatest hands,
I love the ground whereon she stands.

I love my love, and well she knows,
I love the ground whereon she goes.
If you no more on earth I see,
I can't serve you as you have me.

The winter's passed, and the leaves are green,
The time is passed that we have seen;
But still I hope the time will come
When you and I shall be as one.

I go to the Clyde for to mourn and weep,
But satisfied I never could sleep.
I'll write to you in a few short lines;
I'll suffer death ten thousand times.

I love my love, and well she knows,
I love the ground whereon she goes.
The prettiest face and the neatest hands,
I love the ground whereon she stands.

So fare ye well, my own true love;
I'll see your face in the stars above.
And still I hope the time will come
When you and I shall be as one.

A Very Flattering Self Portrait, from the Jim and Carolyn Caswell collection. Photo by Gary Bogue.

After the Thunderstorm, from a private collection. Photo by Gary Bogue.

Over in the Meadow

Over in the meadow in the sand in the sun,
Lived an old mother toady and her little toady one.
"Hop!" said the mother. "I hop!" said the one.
So they hopped and were glad in the sand in the sun.

Over in the meadow where the stream runs blue,
Lived an old mother fish and her little fishes two.
"Swim!" said the mother. "We swim!" said the two.
So they swam and they leaped where the stream runs blue.

Over in the meadow in a nest in a tree,
Lived an old mother birdie and her little birdies three.
"Sing!" said the mother. "We sing," said the three.
So they sang and were glad in the nest in the tree.

Over in the meadow in the reeds by the shore,
Lived an old mother duck and her little ducks four.
"Quack!" said the mother. "We quack!" said the four.
So they quacked and they splashed in the reeds by the shore.

Over in the meadow in a snug beehive,
Lived an old mother bee and her little bees five.
"Buzz!" said the mother. "We buzz!" said the five.
So they buzzed and they hummed in the snug beehive.

About the Artist

On Top of Old Smoky features the distinctive artwork of Linda Anderson. Her paintings in this book are rendered in two different mediums. While most of the pieces are done in oil paints on Belgium linen canvas, the other paintings, which have an almost Haitian flair, are rendered in oil crayons on fine-grit sandpaper.

Anderson's entire life has been spent in Clarkesville, Georgia, a tiny Appalachian town, where she has worked as both a carpenter and a licensed practical nurse. In the spring of 1982, while nursing her invalid teenage daughter, Anderson began to paint. The following autumn, she took her first twenty canvases to a local arts and crafts fair, and in less than a year, she held her first art show at Alexander Gallery in Atlanta.

Since that time, Linda Anderson's magnificent artwork has been exhibited in galleries all over the United States, such as America's Folk Heritage Gallery in New York City and the San Francisco Craft and Folk Art Museum. *On Top of Old Smoky* is her first book.

"When we were children we walked a good distance through thick woods to school. I wish you could have seen those woods in spring. Every dark spot was lit up by dogwood in bold bloom. They seemed to say, 'Walk this way,' and 'Come here, I've lit the path for you.' We'd bring armloads for our teacher. The school would be filled with their blooms. I think children can learn better when they have pretty things to see."

—Linda Anderson